This Book Belongs to :

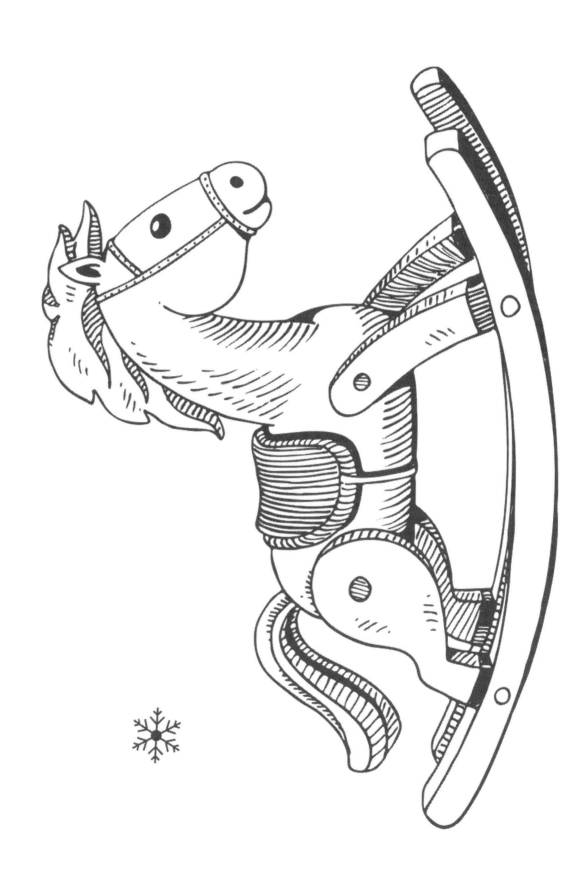

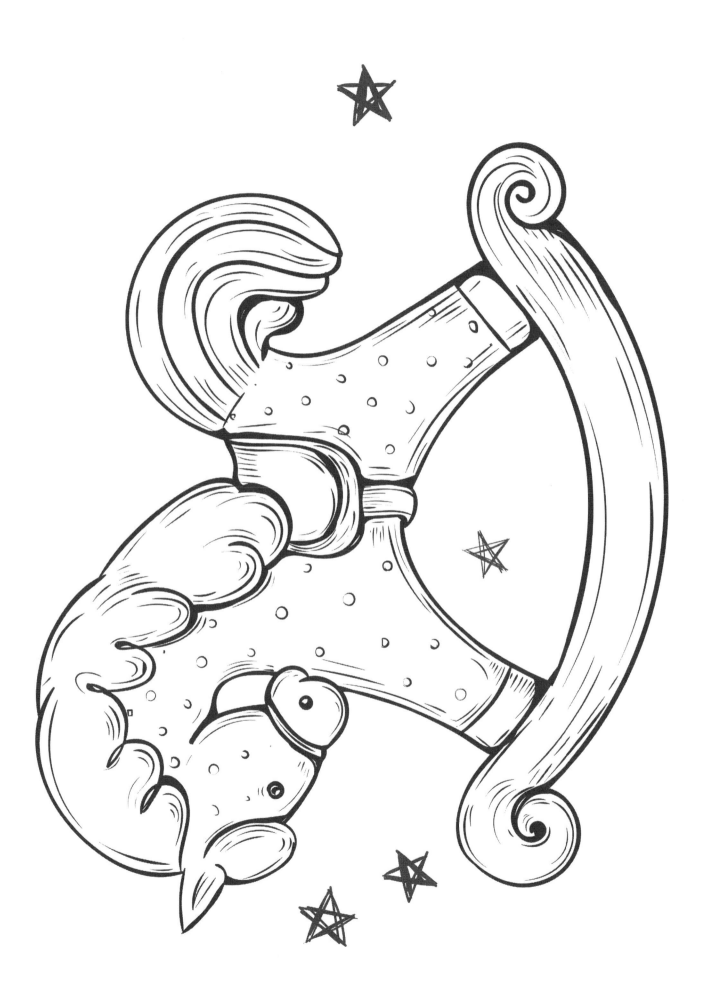

Bonus Game

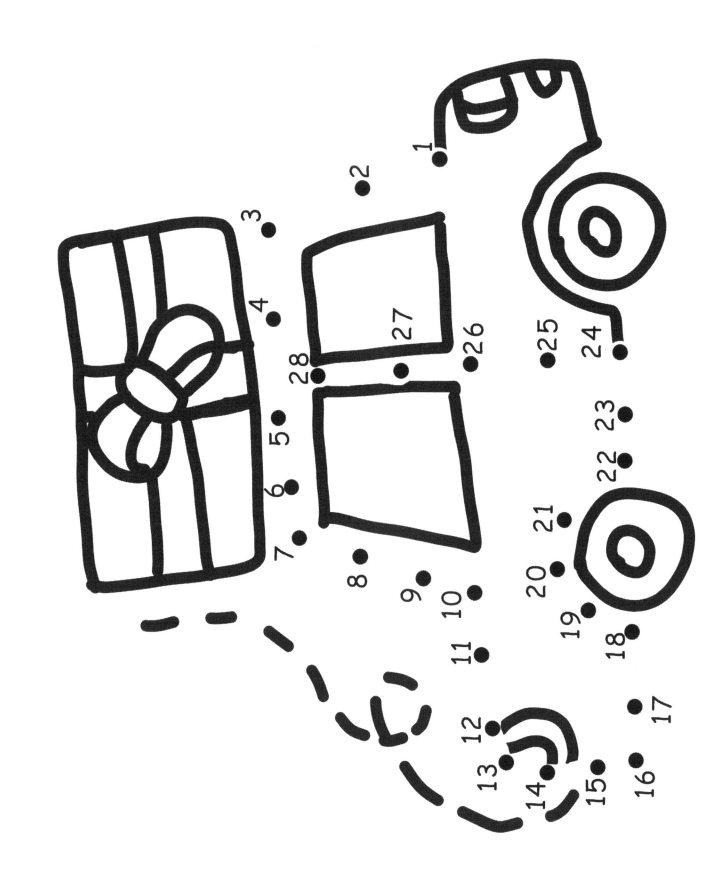

Kids' Activity Workbook Subscribe

Get New Update,
Book Giveaway,
Free Book for Kids
and Promotion

http://bit.ly/act_book_4_kids

MORE KIDS' ACTIVITY BOOKS FROM US
https://k-imagine-pub.com/

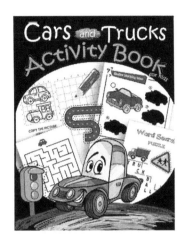

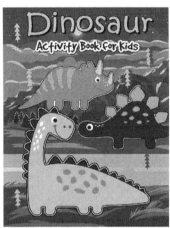
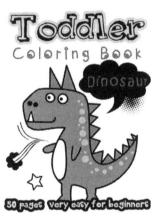

Made in the USA
Columbia, SC
02 December 2019

84153177R00061